Adonis

The Story of a Black Vulture

Illustrator and Storyteller - Jayne Lakhani
Author - Wendy Jones

All rights reserved. Published by BigAppleRed, LLC.
First publication printed in Apache Junction, Arizona

This book is based on true events, and the thoughts of the illustrator and author.

ISBN - 13: 978-1540839473
ISBN - 1540839478

"Start by doing what's necessary;

then do what's possible;

and suddenly you are doing the impossible."

- Francis of Assisi

I am a black vulture, and my job is to fly high in the sky looking for carcasses. I am fiercely loyal to my family and am known for sharing food and shelter with others.

The feathers on my body are so black they sometimes look blue, and I have white stars under my wingtips. My head is grey, my feet are white, but they have no feathers so that I stay clean when I eat.

Years ago I had an accident that left me unable to fly. I'm still not sure how old I was, or exactly how it happened, but half of my right wing is missing.

My parents stayed with me while I recovered.
When it was time for them to leave and join
the others to look for food, I was sad!

Before they flew off, they told me the only
way I would survive on the ground was
to adapt to my environment and to
find my ability in my disability.

The night they left I was scared and lonely!

I found a hollowed out tree stump
and made a nest...my new home.

The next day,
I woke up excited to be alive
and very hungry!

There is a restaurant near my nest.
For days I watched people come and go,
but no one dropped any food.

Late at night I would go dumpster diving,
but the lid was always closed!

I was about to give up when I saw cats
eating scraps behind the restaurant.
Once they left, I hopped over and scavenged.

It wasn't long before I was eating with the cats. One night, a lady surprised us by bringing more food. The cats scurried off.

My instincts told me to fly! Since flying was no longer an option, I did the next best thing. I spread my one and a half wings and made a big hissing snort, "Wheetsh".

She laughed, so I did it again, "Wheetsh". Then she smiled and walked back into the restaurant.

Most of the scraps I eat are fruits or vegetables and sometimes cat food.
I can eat almost anything now, but I really miss my normal food, carrion.

I ate a caterpillar once, but had to spit it out because it scratched my throat.
Then he wiggled away.

It's been over seven years since I met the lady that feeds the cats, and a lot has changed.

By living on the ground, I had to learn to get along with animals, birds and insects.
Many of them have become my friends.

Red the Cardinal comes in the spring and stays for most of the summer. Fraidy the Cat is always around, and Poe the Possum comes and goes during the night.

Ma and Pa still visit every year. They arrive in January and leave in the summer.

I sure wish I could sit in the tree with them!

While they are in the woods, they build a nest on the ground, and Ma lays one or two eggs.

Sometimes they let me help by sitting on the eggs to keep them warm.

When my siblings hatch, they are white, fluffy and really cute.

Everyday I would wait by the side of the
road to see the lady before she went to work.
She would "shoo" me back across the road.

Now I just hang out in the woods with my friends,
and she calls for me when she comes to visit.
"Adonis, where are you beautiful bird?"

Occasionally, the lady brings me things
to keep me busy. My favorite is the rope,
I like throwing it around. Then I run and hop
and make my "Wheetsh" noise.

I also like anything that is shiny or red,
like painted fingernails and toes.
I peck at them with my beak.

Other days we play chase or I take
her on a walk to show her how
the woods have changed.

Flying high above the ground is exhilarating,
but living on the ground has taught me
how to overcome daily challenges.

This is my 'happy strut' and I do it everyday,
because everyday is a new opportunity to learn.

Thank you

A special thank you to Ray, my friends, and customers who have supported my passion for Adonis. His ability to adapt to a life on the ground, and learn to survive under the most trying of circumstances continues to inspire me.

Your unwavering support of my dreams, my art and most of all for your patience in listening to my stories gives me purpose. Adonis has shown me the true meaning of trust and has reinforced my belief that we all can soar like eagles, even if we cannot fly.

Jayne

Made in the USA
Columbia, SC
04 August 2021